AEI LEGISLATIVE ANALYSES
Balanced analyses of current proposals before the Congress, prepared with the help of specialists in law, economics, and government

Proposals for a Biennial Budget

1983

98th Congress
1st Session

AMERICAN ENTERPRISE INSTITUTE
FOR PUBLIC POLICY RESEARCH
Washington and London

S

The legislative analysis program is funded in part by a grant from the Charles E. Culpeper Foundation, Inc.

ISBN 0-8447-0251-X
Legislative Analysis No. 36, 98th Congress
October 1983

CONTENTS

1

INTRODUCTION

The scene is repeated almost every year: Congress nears its recess without approving all thirteen appropriations bills or a continuing resolution to maintain current funding levels. Because the government technically runs out of money if funding is not legislated, federal workers must begin to plan for a possible shutdown—a surprisingly costly procedure. Meetings are canceled, travel is curtailed, and computer programs for splitting government checks are written. When the dreaded first day of the funding gap arrives, employees usually report to work and talk of little but the financial crisis while Congress rushes to complete work on a continuing resolution.

Budget delays are obviously wasteful; yet they are difficult to avoid with the present budget timetable. Although the Congressional Budget and Impoundment Control Act of 1974 (P.L. 93-344) increased the period for consideration of the budget from six to nine months, Congress is still unable to complete its work on time. In his testimony before the Senate Budget Committee, Senator Wendell H. Ford (D-Ky.) of the Rules and Administration Committee has said:

> It has been my experience that our present budget process has become increasingly unrealistic. The annual appropriations process was not working prior to the enactment of the Congressional Budget Act of 1974, and the additional requirements established by that Act have made things worse. The pretense of acting as though it does work costs us dearly in time, money, and effort, but the greatest cost may be incalculable, the cost of poor decisions, made in haste, with inadequate consideration of the need or the consequences. The time has come for us to accept the realities that in our complex modern society, government economic planning, budgeting, and appropriations simply cannot be done constructively in a twelve month period.[1]

To give Congress adequate time for consideration and oversight of the budget, Senator Ford, along with Senators Thad Cochran (R-Miss.), Dan Quayle (R-Ind.), and William V. Roth, Jr. (R-Wis.), and Representative Leon E. Panetta (D-Calif.), has proposed expanding the budget timetable from one year to two years. Alice Rivlin, former director of the Congressional Budget Office, has also thrown her support behind a two-year budget cycle. Others are not so sure that the benefits of such a plan would outweigh the drawbacks. Senator Charles H. Percy (R-Ill.) has said that a shift to a two-year budget cycle would be "a defacto deferral of a share of our Constitutional responsibilities to control the purse-strings."[2] Furthermore, "mandating a radical change in the scope or the timetable of the process could lead to its collapse," warns Robert Reischauer, senior vice-president of the Urban Institute.[3] This legislative analysis examines several bills to change the budget cycle from one to two years and summarizes the arguments for and against the adoption of such a measure.

2

BACKGROUND

The Constitution gives Congress the power to appropriate money and levy taxes. Moreover, the federal government cannot spend or raise money unless Congress gives it the power to do so. Congress spends money through a two-step procedure composed of authorizations and appropriations.

Authorizations are acts of Congress that establish or continue federal programs or agencies. Authorization bills are the responsibility of the standing committees of Congress and can be annual, multiyear, or for an indefinite period. Although authorization bills may set limits on budget authority, they do not generally legislate funding.[4] Appropriations, which grant budget authority, have by tradition followed authorizations; however, there have been cases where appropriations have preceded authorizations. The Appropriations committees consider and report thirteen appropriations bills to Congress, which attempts to pass them before the beginning of the fiscal year. Most entitlement programs have permanent appropriations, and funds are available for them without current action by Congress.

After appropriations have been passed, the executive, legislative, and judicial branches of government can obligate their funds to payrolls and contracts. Outlays are recorded when the goods and services are actually paid for. Usually outlays lag behind appropriations by a considerable period because of the time taken to obligate funds. Outlays can also be quite unpredictable, because for some multi-year appropriations it is difficult to forecast when the funds will actually be spent.

The Office of Management and Budget provides guidelines to agencies to assist them in spending more evenly over the outlay period. In addition, 1982 legislation requires an appropriation available for obligation for a definite period to be "apportioned to prevent obligation or expenditure at a rate that would indicate a necessity for a deficiency or supplemental appropriation for the period."[5]

Before the passage of the Budget Act of 1974, Congress focused its attention on individual appropriations rather than on outlay, revenue, and deficit totals. This made it easier to legislate new programs without worrying about their effect on the deficit. Because President Nixon thought the appropriations process had become unmanageable, he refused to spend money already appropriated by Congress. The president's power to impound funds was subsequently challenged in court, but, before the cases could be resolved, Congress moved to restrict impoundment legislatively. The Budget Act of 1974 requires the president to inform Congress when funds have been impounded and then to release the funds if a

TABLE 1

TIMETABLE FOR THE CONGRESSIONAL BUDGET PROCESS: CONGRESSIONAL BUDGET AND IMPOUNDMENT CONTROL ACT OF 1974

Deadline	Action to Be Completed
15th day after Congress convenes	President submits his budget along with current services estimates
March 15	Committees submit views and estimates to Budget committees
April 1	Congressional Budget Office submits report to Budget committees
April 15	Budget committees report first concurrent resolution on the budget to their houses
May 15	Committees report bills authorizing new budget authority
May 15	Congress adopts first concurrent resolution on the budget
7th day after Labor Day	Congress completes action on bills providing budget authority and spending authority
September 15	Congress completes action on second required concurrent resolution on the budget
September 25	Congress completes action on reconciliation process implementing second concurrent resolution
October 1	Fiscal year begins

SOURCE: P.L. 93-344.

resolution of disapproval is passed.[6] More important for this analysis, the act also introduced a formal procedure to make the budget process more orderly and force Congress to consider its spending decisions more carefully.

The 1974 Budget Act calls for Congress to prepare two budget resolutions and gives a timetable for completion of action on the budget (see table 1). The Budget committees use the president's budget and the views and estimates of congressional committees to set spending and revenue targets for the first budget resolution. Congress tries to complete action on all authorization bills for the year by May 15, the target date for passage of the first budget resolution. Soon after Labor Day Congress is expected to complete action on all appropriations bills so that a second budget resolution can be passed by the September 15 deadline. The second budget resolution adjusts the targets given in the first budget resolution and makes the limits binding. These limits can be changed by adding floor amendments or by passing a third resolution. Any measure that exceeds the limits is subject to a point of order. The Budget Act also enables the Budget committees to enforce the spending and revenue ceilings by directing committees to report changes in legislation if spending and revenue totals differ from those in the second budget resolution. This process of reconciliation was not attempted until fiscal year 1981, for two reasons. One, the Budget committees were unwilling to risk being defeated, and, two, the Budget Act scheduled only ten days for preparation of reconciliation instructions after passage of the second budget resolution. Since fiscal year 1981, reconciliation instructions have been included in the first resolution instead of the second. This change has virtually transformed the targets of the first resolution into binding limits, significantly reducing the importance of the second resolution.

3

PENDING BILLS

During the first session of the Ninety-eighth Congress, a number of bills to make the budget process biennial have been introduced. Some of these bills seek merely to adjust the timetable; others propose significant procedural change in addition to adjusting the timetable. Below is a short summary of four of these bills and their calendars.

H.R. 750: BIENNIAL BUDGETING ACT OF 1983

H.R. 750, the Biennial Budgeting Act of 1983, was introduced into the House of Representatives on January 25, 1983, by Representative Panetta. It was referred to both the Rules Committee and the Government Operations Committee.

H.R. 750 emphasizes oversight, reserving a full six months of the first session for oversight hearings in the committees. The measure eliminates the second budget resolution and spreads out consideration of the single budget resolution and authorizations over both sessions. The scheduled dates for completion of all authorization bills and of the budget resolution are March 10 and March 31 of the second session, in that order. After March 31 the Appropriations committees meet to consider bills providing new budget authority for the two-year period. The deadline for reconciliation is September 25, although work on a reconciliation bill can begin any time after the passage of the resolution. In fact, reconciliation instructions may be included in the budget resolution. The changes authorized by this legislation would take effect on the first day of the first session of the Ninety-ninth Congress.

Table 2 shows the proposed timetable for budget action under H.R. 750.

S. 12 AND S. 95: BUDGET PROCEDURES IMPROVEMENT ACT OF 1983

Senator Ford is the primary sponsor of S. 12, the Budget Procedures Improvement Act of 1983. Senators Quayle, Dale Bumpers (D-Ark.), Claiborne Pell (D-R.I.), Sam Nunn (D-Ga.), Jake Garn (R-Utah), Walter D. Huddleston (D-Ky.), Steven D. Symms (R-Idaho), Nancy L. Kassebaum (R-Kans.), J. James Exon (D-Nebr.), and Paul E. Tsongas (D-Mass.) are listed as cosponsors of the measure, which was introduced on January 26, 1983. S. 12 was referred to the Budget, Governmental Affairs, and Rules and Administration committees. S. 95, an identical bill, was introduced by Senator Quayle, with Senators Ford and Kassebaum as cosponsors.

S. 12 retains both budget resolutions, with the first budget resolution and authorizations due in the first session and the second budget resolution and appropriations in the second session. The two-year budget period would begin on October 1 of even-numbered years. The bill makes two major changes in procedure: (1) only the second resolution can be used for reconciliation, and (2) no

---

TABLE 2

PROPOSED TIMETABLE FOR THE CONGRESSIONAL BUDGET PROCESS:
BIENNIAL BUDGETING ACT OF 1983

Deadline	Action to Be Completed
First session	
January 3	President submits current services budget
15th day after Congress meets	President submits his budget for two-fiscal-year period beginning in succeeding calendar year (the 'two-fiscal-year budget period')
	All committees begin oversight hearings with respect to two-fiscal-year budget period
June 30	Committees complete oversight hearings and submit their reports thereon
July 1	All committees begin legislative work for two-fiscal-year budget period
October 31	Committees and joint committees submit reports to Budget committees with respect to two-fiscal-year budget period
November 10	Congressional Budget Office submits report to Budget committees with respect to two-fiscal-year budget period
November 30	Budget committees in both houses report first concurrent resolution on budget for two-fiscal-year budget period
December 31	Committees report bills and resolutions authorizing new budget authority and providing new spending authority for two-fiscal-year budget period
Second session	
January 3	President submits current services budget
15th day after Congress meets	President submits revised budget for two-fiscal-year budget period

Table continues

TABLE 2 (continued)

Deadline	Action to Be Completed
March 10	Congress completes action on bills and resolutions authorizing new budget authority and providing new spending authority for two-fiscal-year budget period
March 31	Congress completes action on concurrent resolution on budget for two-fiscal-year budget period
April 15	Appropriations Committee reports bills and resolutions providing new budget authority for two-fiscal-year budget period
7th day after Labor Day	Congress completes action on bills and resolutions providing new budget authority and new entitlement authority for two-fiscal-year budget period
September 25	Congress completes action on reconciliation bill or resolution, or both, implementing concurrent resolution
October 1	Two-fiscal-year budget period begins

SOURCE: 98th Congress, 1st session, H.R. 750, "Biennial Budgeting Act of 1983."

final action on bills providing new spending or new budget authority can be taken until after the second resolution and reconciliation are completed. The time for preparation and consideration of reconciliation is extended from August 1 to September 25, instead of the ten-day period provided in existing legislation. Currently the first budget resolution is used for reconciliation, and spending legislation cannot be passed until completion of the first budget resolution unless a waiver is approved to allow for earlier consideration. The bill would also increase the allowable time for debate on reconciliation from 20 to 100 hours. All regular appropriations acts would be enacted for a two-fiscal-year budget period and would specify the amount of appropriations provided for each fiscal year in that period.

The act also modifies and strengthens oversight activities by requiring congressional committees to review and study laws and programs under their jurisdiction to determine whether they should be continued, modified, or eliminated. These oversight reports would be due on October 1 of each even-numbered year and would form the basis for the committee's legislative work in the succeeding Congress.

The provisions of this act would take effect on the first day of the Ninety-ninth Congress. Table 3 shows the timetable for budget action as proposed in S. 12 and S. 95.

TABLE 3

PROPOSED TIMETABLE FOR THE CONGRESSIONAL BUDGET PROCESS:
BUDGET PROCEDURES IMPROVEMENT ACT OF 1983

Deadline	Action to Be Completed
First session	
November 10 (of preceding year)	President submits current services budget for two-fiscal-year budget period beginning in the succeeding even-numbered year
January 15	President submits his budget for two-fiscal-year budget period beginning in the succeeding calendar year
April 15	Congressional Budget Office submits report to Budget committees with respect to two-fiscal-year budget period
May 15	Committees and joint committees submit reports to Budget committees with respect to two-fiscal-year budget period
June 15	Budget committees report first concurrent resolution on the budget for two-fiscal-year budget period to their houses
July 1	Committees report bills and resolutions authorizing new budget authority for two-fiscal-year budget period
July 31	Congress completes action on first concurrent resolution on the budget for two-fiscal-year budget period
September 15	Committees report allocations of first concurrent resolution on the budget among programs within their jurisdiction
December 1	Congress completes action on bills and resolutions authorizing new budget authority for two-fiscal-year budget period
Second session	
January 15	President submits revised budget for two-fiscal-year budget period
March 31	House committees report bills providing new budget authority and new spending authority for two-fiscal-year budget period

Table continues

TABLE 3 (continued)

Deadline	Action to Be Completed
March 31	Congressional Budget Office submits report to Budget committees with respect to two-fiscal-year budget period
April 15	Senate committees report bills providing new budget authority and new spending authority for two-fiscal-year budget period
June 15	Budget committees report second required concurrent resolution on the budget for two-fiscal-year budget period to their houses
July 15	Congress completes action on bills and resolutions providing new budget authority and new spending authority for two-fiscal-year budget period
August 1	Congress completes action on second required concurrent resolution on the budget for two-fiscal-year budget period
September 25	Congress completes action on reconciliation bill or resolution, or both, implementing second required concurrent resolution on the budget for two-fiscal-year budget period
October 1	two-fiscal-year budget period begins

SOURCE: 98th Congress, 1st session, S. 12 and S. 95, "Budget Procedures Improvement Act of 1983."

S. 20: BUDGET REFORM ACT OF 1983

S. 20, the Budget Reform Act of 1983, was introduced by Senator Roth on January 26, 1983. It was referred to the Budget and Governmental Affairs committees on January 26.

The Budget Reform Act calls for a single budget resolution, although, if necessary, a second resolution could be passed with a two-thirds vote of Congress. Reconciliation is permitted any time after May 31 in the first year, the deadline for completion of the budget resolution. Appropriations, also considered in the first year, are combined from the thirteen separate bills into a single two-year omnibus appropriation bill. The second session would be devoted to oversight and considering authorizations. Besides providing for an omnibus appropriation bill, S. 20 makes one other major procedural change—it incorporates the spending of off-budget agencies into the budget resolution.

Effective January 1, 1986, the two-year fiscal period would begin on January 1 of each even-numbered year and would end on December 31 of each odd-numbered year. (The existing federal fiscal year begins October 1 and ends September 30.) The Office of Management and Budget would be responsible for coordinating an orderly transition to the new two-year fiscal period. The bill would allow each new president and Congress to put their policies in place in the first year of their terms.

The timetable shown in table 4 would take effect beginning with the Ninety-ninth Congress.

TABLE 4

PROPOSED TIMETABLE FOR THE CONGRESSIONAL BUDGET PROCESS:
BUDGET REFORM ACT OF 1983

Deadline	Action to Be Completed
First session	
January 2	Committees submit oversight reports to their respective houses
15th day after Congress meets	President submits his budget for two-year fiscal period beginning in the succeeding calendar year, including current services budget
March 31	Committees and joint committees submit views and estimates to Budget committees with respect to two-year fiscal period
April 15	Congressional Budget Office submits report to Budget committees with respect to two-year fiscal period beginning in January 1 of the succeeding year
April 30	Budget committees report concurrent resolution on the budget for two-year fiscal period to their respective houses
May 15	Committees report bills and resolutions authorizing new budget authority
May 31	Congress completes action on concurrent resolution on the budget for two-year fiscal period
June 15	House Appropriations Committee reports omnibus appropriation bill for two-year fiscal period
July 15	President and Congressional Budget Office report to the Budget committees

Table continues

TABLE 4 (continued)

Deadline	Action to Be Completed
July 31	House completes action on omnibus appropriation bill for two-year fiscal period
7th day after Labor Day	Senate Appropriations Committee reports omnibus appropriation bill for two-year fiscal period
September 30	Senate completes action on omnibus appropriation bill for two-year fiscal period
September 30	Congress completes action on bills and resolutions providing new spending authority for two-year fiscal period
October 15	Congress completes action on omnibus appropriation bill for two-year fiscal period
Second session	
January 1	Two-year fiscal period begins
January 15	President and Congressional Budget Office report to Budget committees
July 15	President and Congressional Budget Office report to Budget committees
During session	Committees conduct oversight on programs and activities within their jurisdiction

SOURCE: 98th Congress, 1st session, S. 20, "Budget Reform Act of 1983."

S. 922: TWO YEAR BUDGETARY PLANNING ACT OF 1983

On March 24, 1983, S. 922, the Two Year Budgetary Planning Act of 1983, was introduced into the Senate by Senator Cochran. It was referred to the Budget and Governmental Affairs committees.

S. 922 does away with the second budget resolution and instead requires Congress to pass a single resolution by May 15 of the first year. Congress is able to make revisions in the resolution with a three-fifths vote in each house. The most interesting feature of this bill is that appropriations are passed on the seventh day after Labor Day in the first year for the first fiscal year of the budget cycle and on the seventh day after Labor Day in the second year for the second fiscal year of the budget cycle. This reduces the time between budget predictions and outlays by several months, which increases the accuracy of the predictions. The act would take effect on October 1, 1984.

Table 5 shows the timetable for budget action as proposed in S. 922.

TABLE 5

PROPOSED TIMETABLE FOR THE CONGRESSIONAL BUDGET PROCESS: TWO YEAR BUDGETARY PLANNING ACT OF 1983

Deadline	Action to Be Completed
First session	
November 10 (of preceding year)	President submits current services budget
15th day after Congress meets	President submits budget
March 15	Committees and joint committees submit reports to Budget committees
April 1	Congressional Budget Office submits report to Budget committees
April 15	Budget committees report concurrent resolution on the budget to their houses
May 15	Committees report bills and resolutions authorizing new budget authority for first fiscal year of two-fiscal-year period
May 15	Congress completes action on concurrent resolution on the budget
7th day after Labor Day	Congress completes action on bills and resolutions providing new budget authority for first fiscal year of two-fiscal-year period
October 1	Two-fiscal-year period begins
Second session	
15th day after Congress meets	President submits proposed revisions in the budget for two-fiscal-year period in progress
May 15	Committees report bills and resolutions authorizing new budget authority for second fiscal year of two-fiscal-year period
7th day after Labor Day	Congress completes action on bills and resolutions providing new budget authority and new spending authority for second fiscal year of two-fiscal-year period

SOURCE: 98th Congress, 1st session, S. 922, "Two Year Budgetary Planning Act of 1983."

4

ISSUES AND ARGUMENTS

The proposed two-year budget cycle would have extensive and far-reaching effects on the budget process. This chapter examines these effects and describes the advantages and disadvantages of a biennial budget.

USE OF CONGRESSIONAL TIME

Over the last twenty years more than seventy-four continuing resolutions have been passed, because action on appropriations bills has not been completed in time. After the Congressional Budget and Impoundment Control Act of 1974 became law, the situation improved temporarily. At the start of fiscal year 1976, the first fiscal year covered by the act, President Ford had signed into law all thirteen appropriations bills. Since that time the lawmakers' record has worsened steadily. Excluding appropriations bills for fiscal year 1984, only 25 percent of appropriations bills since 1976 have been enacted before the start of the fiscal year.[7] The delays have led Alice Rivlin to state: "Experience with the budget process has revealed that there simply is not time between January and September for such a lengthy and iterative process of decision making."[8]

The major reason for budget delays is the simple fact that Congress has more work to do. At the end of World War II, 95 percent of federal spending was permanently authorized; today less than 80 percent of federal spending is permanently authorized.[9] This means that more time is spent looking at a relatively small group of federal funds that have short-term authorizations at the expense of oversight of funds that have permanent authorizations. Although some annually authorized programs may benefit from increased attention, the need for such programs as the U.S. Tax Court and the Bureau of the Mint to be authorized annually is less clear.

With a two-year budget cycle all programs would have as a minimum two-year authorizations and two-year appropriations. This would mean major savings in the time spent in hearings, markup, floor debate, and conference. But the question remains, Would Congress on the whole spend less time on the budget process?

Opponents claim that a two-year budget cycle would require a large number of midcycle revisions to make adjustments for congressional action and changes in economic forecasts. To support this contention, they cite the experience of the Senate Foreign Relations Committee, which was unable to stick with a two-year authorization bill for foreign assistance. Within a year after passing a two-year authorization bill, Congress passed a supplemental appropriations bill to increase budget authority. Although the foreign assistance program is controversial, it is likely that Congress would be forced to make many similar midcycle changes under a two-year budget cycle. Those opposed to the proposal fear that the increased number of revisions will make the biennial budget process as time consuming as the current system. Changes in economic forecasts can have a major effect on program expenditures. In 1982 the Congressional Budget Office estimated that a one-percentage-point change in the unemployment rate would change outlays for unemployment compensation by $5 billion. The same study found that a one-percentage-point change in the inflation rate during 1982 would add $0.5 billion to outlays for automatically and indirectly indexed programs.[10]

BUDGET CONTROL

Appropriations have long been considered one of the best tools for budget control. Walter Olezek, a specialist in American national government at the Congressional Research Service, explains: "By cutting off or reducing funds, Congress can abolish agencies or curtail programs; by increasing funds, it can build up neglected program areas. In either case, it has formidable power to shape program areas."[11] There are, however, two problems with using appropriations for budget oversight. First, appropriations for some entitlement programs, such as social security and Medicare, usually provide permanent authority to spend the receipts of trust funds. If appropriations for entitlement programs are insufficient to fund existing benefit levels, supplemental appropriations must be passed at a later date to make up the difference. Second, according to Allen Schick, professor in the School of Public Policy at the University of Maryland, "Annual appropriations might convey the appearance of potent congressional command over expenditures, but the reality might be a legislative body too hurried to evaluate any portion effectively."[12]

Many feel a two-year budget cycle would help ameliorate this problem. By spending less time on the formal budget process, supporters contend, Congress would have more time for careful examination of programs. And it is widely believed that increased oversight is the only way Congress will be able to cut entitlements and gain control over the rapidly growing deficits. Several of the bills under consideration here stress the importance of oversight activities in congressional committees. S. 12 requires committees to prepare oversight reports that would form the basis for legislative work in the succeeding Congress. Oversight activities are also stressed in H.R. 750 (where six months of the first session are reserved for such activities) and in S. 20 (where the entire second session is devoted to oversight and authorizations).

Opponents claim that a two-year cycle would provide *less* control over program areas. According to Arnold J. Meltsner, professor of public policy at the University of California, Berkeley, a two-year budget cycle would favor established programs over new ones: "Old programs would have an edge over new ones because it would take the newcomer more time to get into the cycle. Generally, old programs have developed constituencies, and a two-year budget . . . would give them appropriate respect and thus an advantage."[13] This situation would be particularly difficult for a new administration or a new Congress elected on the basis of promised legislative reforms.

15

Federal agencies are very much bound by the budget process since they cannot legally spend money until Congress passes appropriations. Because appropriations are usually late, agency budget planners must produce several alternative budgets to reflect possible appropriations levels. If anticipated funding levels turn out to be wrong, a disproportionately large share of the changes must be made in areas in which funding is not tied up in contracts. According to former budget director Maurice Stans, "there is very little flexibility in the budget because of the tremendous number of commitments that are made years ahead." [14]

States, which on the average receive about 22 percent of their budgets from the federal government, experience similar problems. [15] Uncertainty is especially hard to deal with for the twenty-one states in which the legislature meets only every other year. Changes in these states, made either directly through changes in grants to states or indirectly through changes in programs that affect the citizens of the states, often mean that their legislatures must reconvene to formulate a new budget.

Critics point out that funding for many state programs is known well in advance because these programs receive, or are authorized to receive, advance appropriations, advance funding, and forward funding.

Proponents feel that a biennial budget would simplify the budget process for federal agencies and state and local governments. Since appropriations would be known in advance, multiple budgets would become unnecessary. Changes could be phased in with far less disruption than now occurs, because agencies would have more time to anticipate them. Finally, those in favor of the proposal believe a biennial budget would eliminate funding gaps by giving Congress adequate time to complete work on the budget.

Opponents, on the other hand, argue that planning would become more difficult because of the increased number of supplemental appropriations. Charles Bowsher, the comptroller general of the United States, has given testimony to this effect:

> Each time a complicating factor is introduced into the process, it increases in geometric proportions the complexities of executive branch formulation, presentation, and execution of individual budgets.
>
> For example, when the Congress passes a continuing resolution, then later passes an appropriations bill, and still later passes a supplemental appropriation, agencies affected by that action must apportion, allocate, and administer their funds three times for the fiscal year instead of once. [16]

Those against the measure say history has shown that it is likely Congress will always be late in completing the budget. The number of continuing resolutions has been increasing, even with the expansion of the timetable in 1976, and there is no reason to think a biennial budget would have anything more than a temporary effect on this trend. Of course, a biennial budget will prevent funding gaps in off years, but there are less drastic ways to achieve this goal than to alter the timetable radically.

Opponents and proponents of a two-year budget cycle both concede that there are major difficulties in scheduling budget resolutions under a two-year budget cycle, especially when a single budget resolution is used. Three of the four bills analyzed here—H.R. 750, S. 20, and S. 922—would eliminate the second budget resolution. The two Senate bills would require passage of a single budget resolution in May of the first session; H.R. 750 would require passage by March 31 of the second session.

If the budget resolution is scheduled early in the cycle, newly elected officials will have to produce a budget for two years soon after entering office. In the past preparing an annual budget in such a short period has proved to be a tough task for new congressmen and presidents—preparing a biennial budget could increase the burden tremendously.

Placing a budget resolution later in the cycle would also create problems. Newly elected congressmen and presidents would have to wait an extra year before they could make changes in the budget, changes many of them campaigned to make.

H.R. 750 requires passage of a budget resolution in March of the even-numbered year for the fiscal period beginning in October of that year. S. 12 and S.95 would require a resolution passed in September of the even-numbered year for the fiscal year beginning in October of that year. In each case an administration taking office in January 1985 would have to wait almost two years—until October 1986—to implement its budget priorities. S. 20 requires passage of a resolution in May of the odd-numbered year for the fiscal period beginning in January of the next year; S. 922 requires a budget in May of the odd-numbered year for implementation during the fiscal period beginning in October of that same year. Among the bills under consideration here, the lag between the start of a new administration or the first session of a new Congress and the beginning of the new fiscal period varies from five months for S. 922 (most similar to the existing budget timetable) to eight months for S. 20 and twenty-two months for H.R. 750, S. 12, and S. 95.

Although retaining a first and a second budget resolution would solve some of these problems, there is a danger that the procedure could degenerate into an annual budget process. This has been a problem in many states with a two-year budget cycle, most notably in Florida.

Although there are obvious benefits from advanced budgeting, opponents argue that it is difficult to predict economic conditions accurately far enough into the future to make a biennial budget a viable possibility. Currently budget planners are required to make economic projections at least eighteen months in advance; a biennial budget would require assumptions made as much as thirty to thirty-six months ahead. This increase is likely greatly to reduce the quality of the economic forecasts.

The accuracy of forecasts is also highly dependent on the strength of the economy. In nonrecessionary years changes due to erroneous forecasts have accounted for only 15 percent of supplemental appropriations, but during the recession of 1975–1977, 48 percent of supplemental budget authority was a result of economic events.[17] Theoretically, recessions should be no more difficult to predict than booms, but in the real world there are strong political biases to underestimate the duration and depth of recessions. As a result, officials fail to plan adequately for the subsequent increased demand for entitlement programs, such as unemployment compensation and Aid to Families with Dependent Children, and the concomitant decline in tax receipts. In the past Congress has also passed jobs bills and other countercyclical measures designed to stimulate the economy, further increasing the need for supplemental appropriations.

Inflation also causes difficulties for budget planners. Because cost overruns frequently occur during periods of high inflation, agencies typically try to estimate inflation in order to be adequately funded. Since predictions made thirty months in advance are more uncertain than predictions made eighteen months in advance, agency cost estimates for a two-year budget are likely to have an even larger margin of safety added. It must be emphasized that, although these numbers can be used to fill in the appropriate blanks in a biennial budget, their correlation with ultimate spending figures will be poor.

Opponents of a two-year budget cycle question whether the proposal will increase congressional control over the budget process even if oversight is increased. Senator Joseph Biden (D-Del.) explains:

> The most serious problem is that such proposals take the pressure of required action off the Congress. In fact, this is often held up as one of the merits of the proposal—that it will relieve Congress of the current time pressures in dealing with the budget. While I do not enjoy those pressures any more than anyone else, I do not believe the pressures should be relieved. That will only lead to inaction or, worse, backsliding. With a budget action only in the first year of Congress, think of all the mischief we could get into in the second year!
>
> We should not adopt a proposal that would allow us to formulate a budget only once every two years—only half as many votes on deficits, spending and taxes. I do not believe my constituents would sit still for my thinking about the budget only half as much as I do now. There are many things besides the budget that need to be done. But we can find time to do them.[18]

The budget process has been, according to former Senator Edmund Muskie (D-Me.), "an action-forcing mechanism," intended to eliminate delays and encourage the timely completion of various stages of the budget.[19] Congress has almost always used the time allotted for debate of the budget and then a little more. Even the Budget Act of 1974, which by moving the beginning of the fiscal year from July 1 to October 1 expanded the deliberations on the budget from six to nine months, increased the timeliness of the reports only temporarily. For this reason many feel it is doubtful that expanding the budget cycle from one to two years would solve Congress's budget problems. They argue that the delays are caused not by the process but by the decisions that have to be made. The choices Congress faces are extremely difficult, and opponents fear debate on those choices will be extended to fill whatever time is available.

NOTES TO TEXT

1. U.S. Congress, Senate, Committee on the Budget, *Hearings on Proposed Improvements in the Congressional Budget Act of 1974,* 97th Congress, 2d session, September 21, 1982, p. 3, statement of Senator Wendell H. Ford.

2. Senate, Committee on the Budget, *Hearings on Proposed Improvements in the Congressional Budget Act of 1974,* p. 6, statement of Senator Charles H. Percy.

3. U.S. Congress, House of Representatives, Committee on the Budget, *Budget Process Review,* 97th Congress, 2d session, September 14, 1982, p. 5, statement of Robert D. Reischauer, senior vice-president, Urban Institute.

4. Louis Fisher, *Budget Concepts and Terminology: The Appropriations Phase* (Washington, D.C.: Congressional Research Service, November 21, 1974), p. 4.

5. P.L. 97-258, 96 STAT. 929.

6. The Budget Act of 1974 includes two procedures to deal with impoundments. For impoundments that only defer spending, the Congress can force the president to release the funds if either house passes a resolution calling for their expenditure. For impoundments that terminate programs or cut total spending, Congress would have to pass a rescission bill within forty-five days to rescind appropriations on those programs. If no such rescission bill is passed, the president must spend the funds. The act requires the president to notify the Congress if funds have been impounded.

In recent years the Congress has moved away from the use of the one-house veto of a budget deferral, and the recent Supreme Court decision holding the legislative veto illegal prohibits this method of funds management. It appears that the administration has reached an informal agreement with the Congress to include budget deferrals as part of a legislative package. The deferrals would thus be subject to normal legislative procedures, and the issue of a legislative veto could be avoided.

7. Allen Schick, "Budgeting," in Norman J. Ornstein, Thomas E. Mann, Michael J. Malbin, and John F. Bibby, *Vital Statistics on Congress, 1982* (Washington, D.C.: American Enterprise Institute, 1982), p. 156.

8. U.S. Congress, Senate, Committee on Governmental Affairs, *Hearings on the Budget Reform Act of 1982,* 97th Congress, 2d session, August 19, 1982, p. 3, statement of Alice M. Rivlin, director, Congressional Budget Office.

9. Ibid., p. 6.

10. Congressional Budget Office, *How Changes in Fiscal Policy Affect the Budget: The Feedback Issue* (Washington, D.C.: Congressional Budget Office, June 1982), p. 73.

11. Quoted in Michael D. Margeson, *Approaches to Biennial Budgeting: An Overview* (Washington, D.C.: Congressional Research Service, 1979), p. 12.

12. Ibid., p. 14.

13. Arnold J. Meltsner, "Budget Control through Political Action," in Aaron Wildavsky and Michael J. Boskin, eds., *The Federal Budget: Economics and Politics* (San Francisco: Institute for Contemporary Studies, 1982), p. 323.

14. Quoted in Aaron Wildavsky, *The Politics of the Budgetary Process* (Boston: Little, Brown and Company, 1964), p. 13.

15. U.S. Congress, Senate, Committee on Governmental Affairs, *Hearings on S. 20: The Budget Reform Act of 1983,* 98th Congress, 1st session, May 5, 1983, p. 4, statement of John H. Sununu, governor of New Hampshire.

16. Senate, Committee on Governmental Affairs, *Hearings on the Budget Reform Act of 1982,* statement of Charles A. Bowsher, comptroller general of the United States.

17. Congressional Budget Office, *Supplemental Appropriations in the 1970s* (Washington, D.C.: Congressional Budget Office, July 1981), p. 23.

18. Senate, Committee on the Budget, *Hearings on Proposed Improvements in the Congressional Budget Act of 1974,* p. 4.

19. Ibid., p. 1.

AEI Publications

The Economics of Legal Minimum Wages

SIMON ROTTENBERG, editor

Over two dozen contributors to a conference examined a host of empirical issues relating to the effects of minimum wages on teenagers, agricultural workers, and domestic service workers.

534 pp./1981/paper 2198-0 $10.25/cloth 2197-2 $18.25

Minimum Wages and On-the-Job Training

MASANORI HASHIMOTO

Surveying the effects of the 1967 amendments to the Fair Labor Standards Act, the author contends that the minimum wage deprives low-wage earners of an opportunity to learn on the job by making it illegal for them to receive the lower wage that an employer might offer them together with training.

72 pp./1981/paper 3428-4 $4.25

The Federal Antitrust Laws

JERROLD G. VAN CISE

This study presents the major provisions of the antitrust laws and the purposes for which Congress enacted them, together with the ways they have been observed, enforced, and interpreted. In this fourth revised edition, the author takes into consideration changes in the law and recent court decisions that have occurred since the study was last updated, in 1975.

92 pp./1982/paper 3488-8 $4.95

The Political Economy of Deregulation: Interest Groups in the Regulatory Process

ROGER G. NOLL AND BRUCE M. OWEN

"The book's . . . unique contribution lies in the discussion of how regulation can create opponents of deregulation out of opponents of regulation."
Policy Report.

164 pp./1983/paper 3519-1 $7.95/cloth 3520-5 $15.95

• *Mail orders for publications to:* AMERICAN ENTERPRISE INSTITUTE, 1150 Seventeenth Street, N.W., Washington, D.C. 20036 • *For postage and handling, add 10 percent of total; minimum charge $2, maximum $10 • For information on orders, or to expedite service, call toll free 800-424-2873 • When ordering by International Standard Book Number, please use the AEI prefix—0-8447 • Prices subject to change without notice • Payable in U.S. currency only*